Jecolia

Brittany

2

Penelope

4

Gianna

Lily

Lila Belle

HliNtsa

Sophie

9

Yoonju Kim

10

Samantha

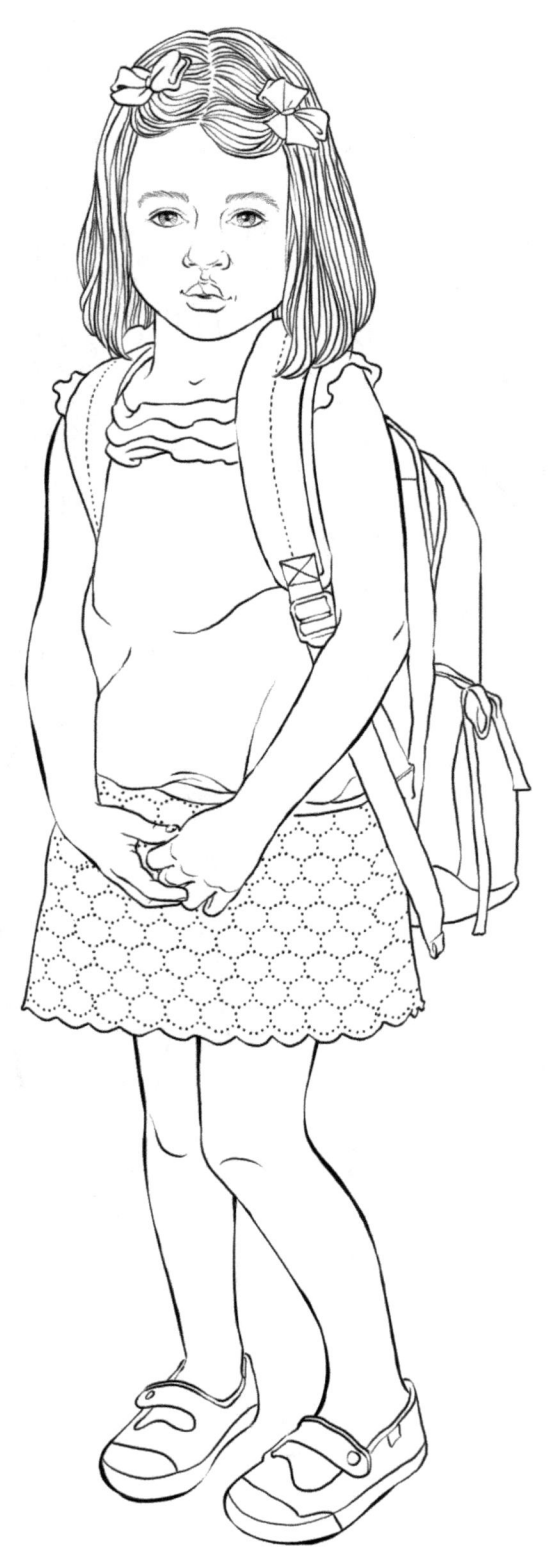

Anna

Taylor

13

Hyo Jin Lee

NEVER
BE
COOL

14

Lorena

15

Ariana

Rashanna

Liliana

Sarah

nica

Jaidyn

Magda

22

23

Kayla

Senautah

25

Mackenzie

Keisha

Jessie

Michelle

Ryanne

Lea

Ari

Carrie ♡

Kia

ተሬሣ

sofia

35

Savannah

37

Lina

Lydia

40

Sooji

Lilli

43

44

Elizabeth

45

Halima

46

Brooke

Evelyn

48

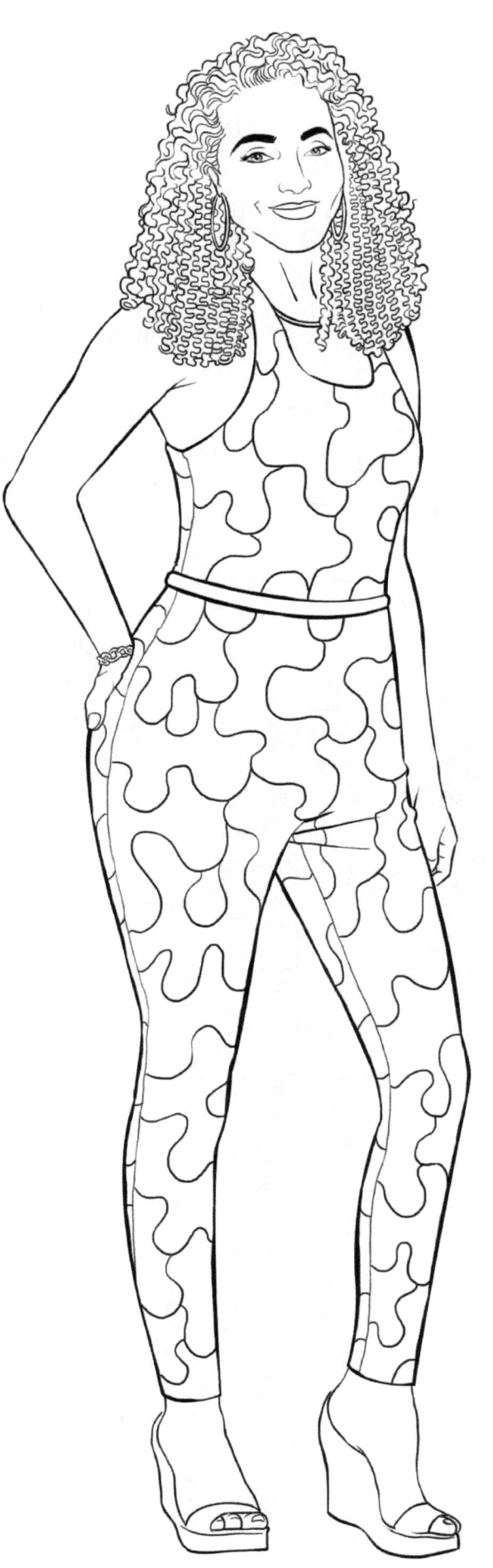

Alejandra

Quinn

Printed in the USA
CPSIA information can be obtained
at www.ICGtesting.com
LVHW061954220823
755997LV00010B/104

Jecolia

Brittany

2

Penelope

4

Gianna

Lily

6

Lila Belle

HliNtsa

8

Sophie

Yoonju Kim

Samantha

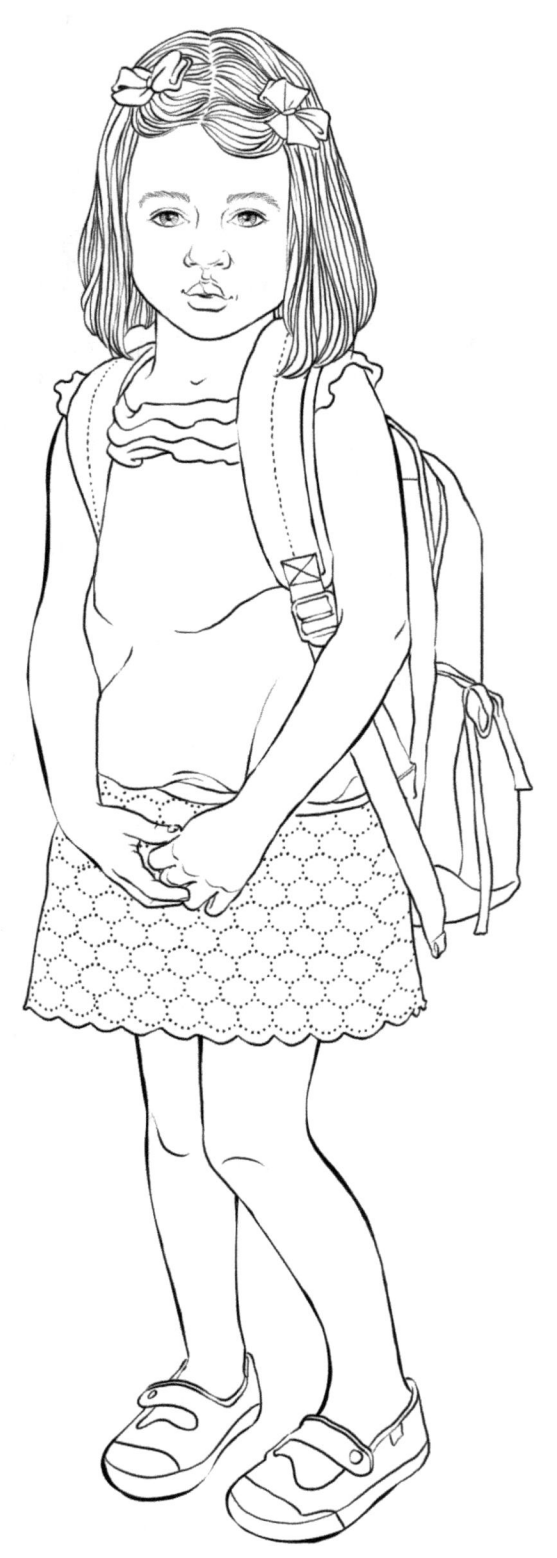

Anna

Taylor

13

Hyojin Lee

NEVER
BE
COOL

14

Lorena

15

Ariana

16

Rashanna

17

Liliana

18

Sarah

nica

20

Jaidyn

21

Magda

22

23

Kayla

Shauna

25

Mackenzie

26

Keisha

27

Jessie

28

Michelle

Ryanne

Lea

Ari

Carrie ♡

33

Kia

34

ተሰሳይ
sofia

35

Savannah

37

Sarah

Lina

Lydia

40

Sooji

Lilli

43

Elizabeth

45

Halima

46

Brooke

47

Evelyn

48

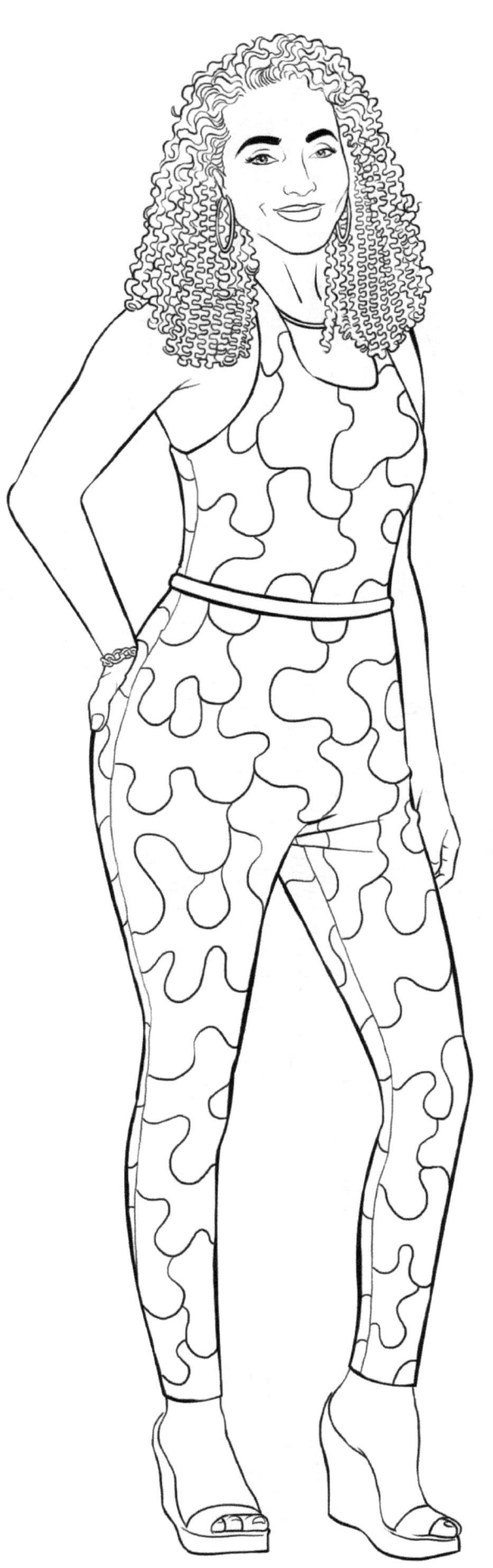

Alejandra

49

Quinn

Printed in the USA
CPSIA information can be obtained
at www.ICGtesting.com
LVHW061954220823
755997LV00010B/104